an/

othered

m/

other

Jem Henderson

Published by Nine Pens

2022

www.ninepens.co.uk

ISBN: 978-1-7398274-7-2

013

Form

Name: [1]

Address.   Street line 1: [2]   Street line 2: [3]

City: [4]

County/State: [5]

Country: [6]

Date of Birth: [7] Place of Birth: [8]

Permission: [9] YES / NO

[1] cut glass / picked out / tentatively / from diamond / *that lie* / smashed underfoot / dust formed into shining new / fragments / you hold it close / try it on each / chapped / finger / knuckles shine pink & swollen / from punching / the wall

[2] this house / this body / *are you home?* / maggot scarred / rimed with salt / willow bent / plumb lined & hard / fragile neck to collar bone / traced with my finger / writing out my name / in your grace

[3] this road / this journey / cool dusk to the mint green of dawn / erase those soft pencil lines / drain / the warm / feathery / light / take them into yourself / in your arms whisper / *it will all be okay* / while the storm / takes the windows / takes the walls

[4] densely pack / unpacked / the forest / deforest / Babel's tower falls / its spire / & domes / you try to understand / grasp their coat / fall / to your knees / as they walk out / the door / leaving we / in the silence

[5] an accounting / state your name / your place of birth / your mother's / maiden name / your shoe size / *that's wrong* / inseam / hands running up / your leg / touching you / where it feels dirty / but / you have no power / *can't* / say no

[6] this swathe of land / pink / our bodies writhe / like earthworms / churning the soil / the cause/way / brown / blue / the endless blue / covered by clouds / too / thunder filled / to ever really know / until the piercing / white pills / tell you / *too late* / your shape / is a lie

[7] you tell me a story / about a haunting / the death of the man / we loved & love / while crickets scream / their lust / along the river / into the dark / rub themselves / to a frenzy / like come-of-age camgirls / pout into the lens / *we're safe in bed* / the only place

[8] Mother / a frightened / startled deer / warm arms / & the hospital bed / she whispers my / *name* / but it changes / between / her lips / & my ear / to something / unknowable / if names have power / then mine is / *the void*

[9] rejection / revolution / we refuse / to tie ourselves / to your forms / morph / like shapeshifters / lift our arms / to the sky / under a waning moon / like wax figures / which we mould / to the shape / of our becoming / we are / multiform

My Mother's Gifting

My mother's father never sees her.
Knowing she is his, his pale body splits
on tracks before a shrieking train.

The gift he leaves stayed with her -
the certainty that she is unloveable.
She trials it out. Married and divorced

already by the time I come. She is 21.
I cry all the time - colic and teeth.
She gives me to her mother for a while,

shifts to the homeless hostel, leaves me
to grow on my own. The gift her father
left her chases through her veins.

I grow. She gathers. We move.
Her bed fills and empties
with twelve men in fifteen years.

We become estranged. The present
in her brain wrapped up, passed on
through the divide. Her clenching hands.

A wooden clog. I bring it to myself
with razor blades and teeth.
I am writing his vengeful gift
into my corpse white flesh.

in sickness and health

when we were ill my mother
would make me and my sister
run up and down the stairs
after she'd called the doctors,
so that when they arrived
the kind man in a bowtie
would know
just how poorly we were.

I asked her, before
the estrangement
how could you do that?
But all she said was
the world is uncaring
It's a mother's job to teach you

My little boy lays in his bed,
the thermometer reading red
The calpol making his chin
sticky and sweet when I kiss him.
He coughs, the sound caught
in his chest like a bird trying to escape

and I put my cool hand
on his hot head
and teach him
it will be okay

Fighting monsters

the red tartan tin held all my Lego
not much - just enough to build a small castle,
      a medium sized helicopter,
          a large tower

the green base the beginning
a hundred different stories
on a cold afternoon
rain humming on the roof
      running down the windows

hiding from raised voices
      muffled cries into a pillow
          the sharp clip of a slap
          around an already swollen face

my sister and I spent hours sorting it into piles
yellow
      red
          white
              black
              blue

From

I am from goldfish from the fair
that live forever or a day

I am from riding the ramps down
to the car park at Morrisons
trolley full of last minute food
that we eat out of date

I am from *Playschool, Fun House,*
Neil Buchanan's floppy Roman bust

From Nanna with her Debenhams for dresses
Marks' for cotton pants in pink multipacks

I'm from coven and clan ruled by
her cigarettes and auburn hair
faded by time and bitter smoke

From the taste of Fruit Salads and Black Jacks
tongue stuck out to show Grandad

I'm from *The Queen's Nose, Sabrina the Teenage Witch*
crushes on all the boys and girls
in *Buffy the Vampire Slayer*

From black clothes, dark sticky lipstick
blonde downy legs at the pool
hiding the rustle of pads in the toilets

when the molecules of me
broke down and away
from the closed door horror of my mother

the apple never falls far

the apple tree blows green leaves
like babies fingers reaching out
to cool clouds who drift by, uncaring

the windows of the houses stare
sightless into the garden
the apple tree shivers
a woman knows she's watched

the rain caressed our skin
barefoot and standing on gravel
spinning around the picnic table
whirl and twist water whipped
rivulets down bare bodies
mother, child, child,
eyes of a peeping neighbour

i was eight, my sister six
we'd never known
this unbound madness
shrill laughter between
rolls of echoing thunder

and yes, an apple tree - or two
one sweet, one tart and tiny
planted from the seed of a granny smith
which mother later swore she'd done

but i remember sneaking out
little hands in rich damp soil
poking a seed into the earth
hoping for something, anything new

the afternoon I lost my virginity
on a single mattress on the floor
in a bungalow with a model
railway in the back garden

at fifteen   I wasn't sure
if losing this   would make me   *woman*
after all   I'd read   Mills and Boon
too   many   nights   alone
touching myself   getting off   on
pillows   the shower head   it
wasn't   enough
this boy   with his blue lined   eyes
glitter   the rough way   he
sang   played guitar
his father's   garden   its
model   railway   he
was danger   it made me   want
him   we listened   to Soft
Cell   kissing   on his
single   bed   I was
frightened   but I didn't want   to
say   in this moment becoming   I
never   told him my first time
the blood on the sheets   that
testament   in the quiet   afterwards
I cried   this *tainted love*   left
me   almost   the same   but
equally
                older

14

Maslow's Hierarchy of Needs according to a 16 year old girl
laying on a single bed staring at the ceiling in a homeless
hostel

i. Physiological

Of the body. Covering. Clothes. Washing powder and fabric
softener.
Bacon, sausage, cheese; enough to gorge on. All those things I
can't afford.
A humming fridge that makes me grin when I open it, more than
just
a dribble in a bottle of milk, a limp lettuce leaf frozen solid to the
back.

ii. Safety

Victorian terraces loom like junkie teeth. Hurry back. Hide from
the police.
From love. A place to go. A place to be. A place to be myself,
away
from the eyes of Moloch and God, whose love burns when I piss.
Lights that turn on. Lights that turn off. I whimper like a child in
the dark.

iii. Belongingness

The weight of you on top, grinning and grinding, sparking like a
welder's arc.
This shrieking congress of sorrows, where sweat or tears rain
down
into my open mouth, tongue out. I am made from spare change,
copper,
cement, endless oil slicked on stone. Light streams onto the wet
bed.

iv. Esteem

My brain decides how much dopamine and serotonin I am
allowed today.
Not much. I am a consciousness without a body. Say it with me.
I am loved. I am enough. Three Hail Marys and the razorblade
slicked out
of the packet, open and ready to show my thighs what they mean
to me.

v. Self actualisation

I am become. From mouldy slices of white bread, the
bloodpocked dents
in plaster, scribbles of poems on final demands, Facebook
notifications
dripping need into my veins, the saline of the sea turned red. Lift
me up
to heaven which is here and exists and is nowhere but the
jailhouse.

an incomplete list of treasures in my horde

yesterday's newspapers / the day before's / the oil slick blue gleam of a magpie's feather / art magazines from graffiti to sculptors that I've never heard of / a hagstone held up to the eye to see the leering skull of my Nanna as she watches me cry / a leaf - red dipped tip fade through orange and yellow / the champagne cork from my wedding day - sliced and holding a silver dollar for longer than I held on my failing marriage / a piece of tissue blotted with tears and red lip print / a keyring won from a 2p machine our last trip to Scarborough / an empty strip of my contraceptive pills / a dead wasp shrivelled on the dusty windowsill / a pile of notebooks - some half filled with lists - *wake up* written at the top / *at least I managed to do something that day* / my teddy from when I was born - a present from my father / the note from the day he left - *I'm sorry, I just don't love you anymore* - not meant for me but for my mother / an empty condom wrapper tucked down the side of my mattress / that first lock of my baby's hair / the baby pink bib she never got to wear

Whum

The echidna is of the Tachyglossidae family,
in the monotreme order of egg-laying mammals.
It's an alien, a mother that shouldn't be.

I go into the doctors surgery
bustled through in coats and seats and smiles
sit on the tissued bed for the cheery midwife
lift my t-shirt for the prod of the doppler
soaking in the *whumwhumwhum* of your heartbeat

a week later, I'm at the maternity unit
surrounded by fat mothers with round bellies
while you escape me, clot by drop
the ultrasound wand meddles my joy
a cataclysm of silence

we go home for pizza, tea, TV
hot water bottles, silence, too many blankets
the adverts show us starving kids in Syria
We watch Roy Walker on reruns of Catchphrase
'It's good, but it's not right'.

gretel

at the back of the garden under the apple tree
where gnarling branches finger fat poison
fruit, the hum of summer bees collect rose-
scented pollen, witch-tricked in sweetness.
small hands gathered the flush of rhubarb,
maiden pink with shame, snapped off, leaf-
whipped for immersion in crumble and
custard, cinnamon for seasoning, sugar to
make the stem sweet, sugar to make the
children sweet, butter to grease them like fat
little pigs, slipping out of the grasp of the
giant. sunday lunch with gravy and
puddings and then comes dessert. *fee fi fo fum*
I smell the blood of an english woman, locked
in the bathroom, hiding from the post sunday
roast wrath, the *old peculiar-* fueled
yorkshireman snarling, echoing the roar of
the engines of the telly as me and my sister
turn up the volume of the formula one while
the crumble blackens in the oven

i give birth to a mouse

a white mouse
where my heart
should be

white like
milk, alive

not like snow

he got in
through the cigar burn
on my chest

where my ash-pale skin
is cratered like the moon

he jitters against
my rib cage

fish him out
my little finger
hooked round
tail

pull

hear the sucking

of the sticky vacuum

clotted fur
flattens
to his
twitching head

Aposematic

When you were born
I dyed my hair green.
Reaching pale shoots
into an unknown dawn.

When you were born
I dyed my hair blue.
A shrieking siren
to let my husband know
how I was feeling.
He tussled it, said *love you*
before leaving the house.

When you were born
I let my hair grow out.
Newborn, milk-soaked
mastitis anxiety.
No idea of night or day
for eight long weeks.

When you were born
I dyed my hair brown,
finally fitting into
the box my mother
made for me.
Are you sure? he said.

When you were born
I dyed my hair red,
flaying myself open.
Love it he said.

mirror // mirror

the shine of moisturiser on my skin // these open pores // the weight of flesh above my eyebrow starting to dance away from its youthful smiling figure // and there she is // my mother // staring at me through twenty years and the mirror in black and white // that poisoned curl of lip //

here she is again // a photo of me and my son // all that care in my face // and she's there in the crease of the crow's feet //

maybe I'm remembering wrong // only the storm clouds // and not the blazing sun // the handprint on my cheek // not the tuck of hair behind my ear // the way her eyes got shiny bright when she knew she caught me in childish lie // her whimpering in the night //

it's not that I think i'm ugly // after all my hair is bright // my lips fuller and pulled to a lopsided smile // it's just that when I see her in the mirror // I can't help but feel // her hand on my throat

Jōmon doki

Jōmon means rope- patterned / describing the indents /
pressed into pale clay /

and you play me / a cat gut stringed viola / fragile
and warm / in the buttery almost-gone daylight /
my body arcing / against black nylon cord / you've
tied me / wrist to wrist /   wrists to bed /

your voice rumbles / low / *good girl* / like the wheels
of a car / on a winding country road / white shirt
sleeves rolled up / hands warmed on the blue supple
curve of my back /

vertebrae a string of pearls / held *just so* by these
knots / *no mercy* / shrieking / begging until you bind
my tongue / my eyes / *God, blind me* / lost in the
harmony of your whispers / your fingers /   your
stubble on my neck

tomorrow / there will be bruises / purple stars
trapped in yellow / across the knot of scars / on my
wrist

In which I compare my father
to the dog that he is

He finds me through the bald headed
landlord of my local pub; sniffs me out like
a bone. The sad faced beagle buys me
a pint, drinks his too fast, lets out a greasy burp.
I've been looking for you forever, he says
although I've been here, waiting in the same spot,

for 18 years. The beagle leaves again,
snuffles his way through town, raising his leg,
etches his mark on lamp post, bin, garden gate.
God, it's such a mess, he says. Finds himself
another bitch, rubbing up on her until he's spent.
She's the most important woman in my life.

I've been drinking and partying and fucking
myself silly. Living alone gives you such free rein
and the absence of the pole star is reason enough
to find yourself lost under a dark sky, in a forest full
of shadows and wolves. The beagle, rheumy-eyed,
sniffs, brings his puppies to the table. Says '*make sure*

you study hard, so you don't grow up to be like that.'
The cry of hounds look at me across the dining room,
tears leaking from my eyes. He cocks his leg up,
scratches behind his ear, frantically shoos me away
from his family, and I, the runt of the litter,
go back to my cold bath flat and howl.

The Moon Speaks

Last night, he snuck in through my window
round and fat, cackling like a magpie.
Grabbed me by my pixie hair, whispered
that he doesn't love me, my mother doesn't,
my child doesn't, how could he when
I'm such a dreadful parent, only playacting
through video games and chalk drawings
of sunshines and rabbits on the pavement.
My mother looks at me, fat cheeked, pig eyed,
smiles her greased smile as I pile up sweets,
custard creams, endless cups of weak black tea,
the skin from my thighs and forearms, Lego
that make up the last cakes of my sanity,
the smile from my face, a million hours of tears,
all on the plate before her and she gobbles it up
a black hole, a void I can't fill until I wake up
sweating, the moon slinking out, back
to his sky and his darkness, leaving me
and my emptied chest with nothing but the
sad cry-catch of tears trapped in my throat.

Wildflower

I collect bindweed from the railway tracks,

great trumpet horn of palest pink.

Commuters gawp through mucky

windows. Blue borage, flowers

star-sweet as stolen honey.

From the river; bulrush and lilies. The blooms

stream rainbows back into the water. For green;

creeping ivy, wound round stems. The milk sap

of sun splurge raises my skin in blushed welts.

Half arranged, I place them in a glass vase,

ready to take to her hospital bed.

At the door to the room, a nurse stops me, bends

her head, inhales, her silver crucifix glinting

in the light. In the white ward,

Mama smiles her half face smile; creased

and still so beautiful, and raises

her crepe paper hands from the blanket.

Munchausen

your mouth smiles now   serves its usual
snide comments   barbed niceties   seeded
throughout   until the doctor comes then it's
slack   like dying tubers   shrivelled in their
holes   your voice feebled   with the
performance   you'll reveal yourself eventually
the kerning slides like your face   into place
your voice comes back to argue ... *don't worry*
you'll receive your Oscar

O dark mother   O black widow   O angel
of the   hospital bed   the micro clots in
your sticky blood work their way through the
fields   plough through vascular rows   idle
before the big return   when you'll win   the
prize for your performance   the endless
               silence of your family

Deer

my mother is a deer -
a muntjac, coming up
to just above my knee.
soft, easily startled, shiv-horned

      she prefers to be alone, or
      gives the impression
      that she prefers to be alone.

i open the text without looking at the sender
i hear that you are pregnant, congratulations! Xx

          a shake of ice and spite across my shoulders

i can feel myself trembling but i can't see it
i've not thrown my phone across the room
only because i don't want to break it

      there's something in my throat
      stopping the air from coming out
      a lump of all the words I've never said
      responding to her barks -
      she's very loud
      given she's only yay high

i flex my thumbs and type in a way
i'll be able to feel for years thinking back to this moment -

who knew that joints could hold memories?

i'm sorry that you found out. when my baby is born, I'm telling ~~him~~
them

> (keep it gender neutral,
> even though at 25 weeks along
> your boy is growing -
> the size of a puffball mushroom)

I'm telling them you are dead

these green hills of

England / overcast sky pregnant with
the applause of rain / traipse the hills / valleys / ginnels
/ alleys / trample the causeway with the heavy feet of
slaves / white filthy feet / made indelible with silt / full
of muck / earthworms / fossils / ceramic / the broken
bodies of a hundred fertility goddesses buxom and fat
with child / stem the flow / shout back the tide / my
body is not an accident / on purpose I've filled it with
men and cum / filled with boy child / expelled / impelled
/ into arms that squeeze

the storm rumbles / the cause of this
thickened air / promising retribution / our foundations
have already been built / stamped with the feet of our
ancestors / a glass of spilled milk / an empty bottle of
pills /   the pencil sketches of a genius / writing
backwards in the mirror / the wall-eyed ramble of the
village witch / the scathing tongue of my mother who
says *no one will love you* /

Function

(to be cut out and pasted in the order that you deem fit.

(Or not.))

X. crimson painted / crusted / lips apart / sotto voce / *take these chromosomes / and make them dance like paupers / desperate for a coin or two*

> 1. *at last... /* we rare / as desert flood / our rivers run / red with viscid blood / spill life / in those crevasses / where no one thinks to look

> 2. take all the parts / lay them down on the sticky floor / just to check / *are you all there? / is there something you want from me?*

3. heart / liver / lung times two / pancreas / kidneys / to
let the water out / eyes / to let the water out / the love of a
good parent / or a deep relentless trauma

Y. I've framed my life / my body / my sex / around what men
want / when what they want / is the same as women / *an end to all
this / let the binary fall apart / may a hundred genders bloom*

> A.   a hand span, multiplied to build
> the height of horses / your arm
> span is usually the same as your
> height / your foot length marks
> your forearm / all these bits of
> other bits / the human body / is
> synecdoche
>
> B. this fixed form, immutable,
> carved stars in ancient jade / a
> false form of me, built up in my
> mother's head / relentlessly
> destroyed from the age of nine
> by all these sticky wants and

needs and emotions / that didn't
mirror hers at all / her womb, a
tomb for the cave shadow I
become

C. no one will ever love me

no one will ever love me

D. decay exists as a tacit form of life / shrinking and grieving /
growing and sprouting / no longer breathing / our spores spat
like watermelon seeds from your mouth / mycelium corridors
and halls / lichen temples with fungal altars and ash bowers /
dervish whirls and eddies, whorls and succour / worship what we
would have been

The Locked Box

Under the bed, hidden behind
dust balls, lost clothes, sex toys.
I keep my thoughts of you
triple locked with box, bolt and bar.

Time corrodes the padlock open.
You escape, a naked runaway
lonely child. Slip out into the darkness,
shackles off and milk teeth bared.

Your skinny lips pursed, painted peach.
Black catsuit clings, crowing *aren't I slim*
even after two teenage daughters,
c-section scar covered by the zip.

Your telephone voice, no Bradford *ee*,
higher and softer than the spite
of spat commands, admonishments.
Catch-throat sobs at night, another lost love.

Your head looks tiny when you screech,
pig eyes shrunk tight, a list of reasons
why I'm a terrible daughter.
You hold out your arms and cry.

We haven't spoken in eight years.
You've never met my child.
I'm scared, because of you,
he'll need a box of his own.

if you had a clear skull

i wonder if I'd be able to see your thoughts - the fuzz of apricots &
the buzzing of fat wasps & the look of sticky juice dripping down
my chin & the circle splash of blood on the pavement spread-
stretching fingers out to every house on the street & the
bowl spilled across the table & life flickering by like an old
television show & the bounce of the apple across the kitchen
floor & the bruise that makes the cherry soft underneath &
the bruise that makes the brain soft underneath & the crack of
your head as it hits the step like it is made of glass & the spark
of thoughts as they glitch through your broken meat & grapes fat
and green & the table that goes across your knees & the white &
yellow of the gerberas & the green & black of the monitor gone flat

Sestina for a body

Look in the mirror. Pull in tight. Hold my breath.
Stand up straight. Put my hand on my body,
try to love what she sees. Me. This is my shape,
the slow still before the storm, ready and ripe,
an apricot with its pale fuzz and centre stone.
Our delicate flesh. Turn, look at the other

side. Flex these arms. Scars that whisper Mother.
My baby sailing through water. His first breath.
His first, fat laugh. First words. First walk, stone
in his shoe. Maybe that's the lesson, his body
sore from unexpected pain. Life's ripe
with falling cherry blossom. Aches. The shape

it might take. We don't know. This is parenting, shaping
life. Castles. Spaceships. *Power Rangers*. Other
pieces of my childhood I share. Those I won't. Gripe
water soothes an ache. Croup - he can't catch his breath
so I do, a butterfly net. Put it back in his body.
We're the same. Dale-bred. Made of stone.

Of heather. Yellow gorse. Scarborough rock and Yorkshire grit.
Rundown seafronts. 200 acres of parkland. Wanting to escape
my mother's house. Her twisted mouth. My body.
Leave it all behind. Reject this femininity. Become Other.
Love in a way that would leave me disinherited. Her breath
on my neck. My fingers run down her body. Her ripeness.

I dedicate myself to her pain. Kiss it away. Ripe
feelings ready to spill like juice from that apricot. Stone
hearted though, don't forget. Words murmured under my breath.
I love you in secret. That's fine, we're in good shape.
This is fine. Good friends want to kiss each other.
Under the duvet I think about her body.

Us laying together. Her soft, unscarred stomach. My body,
the shipwreck of my motherhood. How I get her to swear, ripe
language colouring the air above my bed like pink smoke. Other
ways I'd like to love her, holding hands with my boy. Stoned
conversation on a Sunday morning. Coloured shapes
of Lego, long walks in the cold where I can see our breath.

Stone butch and femme entwined. The poetry of our bodies.
Us both ripened from trauma to meet ourselves. The shape
of our lives. Older. Other. Until our final breath.

Acknowledgements

Form first appeared in Queer Peers zine from Feeling Queer, a peer support organisation.

Fighting Monsters first appeared in UP! Magazine.

Whum first appeared in Full House Literary Magazine.

Aposematic first appeared in the Hair Raising anthology from Nine Pens Press.

In which I compare my father to the dog that he is, Wild Flower, and The Locked Box appeared in Dreich.

The Moon Speaks appeared in Drawn to the Light Magazine.

Maslow's Hierarchy of Needs... first appeared in the Creative Future Awards Anthology Essential.